AMBLE

AMBLE

POEMS

GUY CRAIG

THOUGHTS ON THE GOOD LIFE PRESS
Oregon, USA

AMBLE

Published by

THOUGHTS ON THE GOOD LIFE PRESS

Portland, Oregon

www.ThoughtsOnTheGoodLife.com

© Copyright 2021 by GUY CRAIG;

Poetry

Written by GUY CRAIG

Artwork by GUY CRAIG

Cover Art by SARAH CRAIG

First Edition

For inquires, write to the author, with the subject line "Inquires," at the email address below.

Hello@ThoughtsOnTheGoodLife.com

Visit - GuyCraigPoetry.com

This book is a work of fiction. Names, characters, places, and incidents either are the product of the author's imagination or are used fictitiously, and any resemblance to actual persons, living or dead, events, organizations, or locales is entirely coincidental.

ISBN: 978-1-7334968-3-4

For Sarah and Kenneth

CONTENTS

Setting I: Morning

Amble 4
I Long for the Rain 5
On My Way 6
Youth-On-Age 7
Potted Umbellularia Californica 8
Iris and Home 9
On the Mountain 11
I Never Tire of This View 12
Hope of Morning 13
At Our Best 14
Conduits 15
Home and Away 16
Infused Path 17

CONTENTS

Setting II: Afternoon

The Complementary Path 21
Wind Chimes 22
Inspiration is a Spirit 24
You Like Me As I Like You 25
With a Kiss 26
Healed 27
Douglas Fir 28
Bouquet of Nettles 29
Moss Over Wood Ash 30
A Good Place for Lunch 31
The Deeply Hurt Often Fight in Chaos 32
Life is Precarious 33
Change of Heart 34
Flooded Bay 35
Balance 36
Old Dog in the River 37
Broadleaf Dock 39
Pruned Branches 40
Word Farming 41
Salmonberry and the Next Idea 42
Thimbleberry 43
Measure of Loss 44
No Trace 45
A Stop at the Dock 46

CONTENTS

Setting III: Evening

My Favorite Gift 49
Red, Warm Glare 50
The Gate 51
Ties of Freedom 52
Summer Reflection 53
Windfall 54
Unpaid Carers 55
When We Help 56
Myrtle Trees 57
Who is Watching the Waves? 58
Returning to the Earth 60
Bald Mountain Meteorite 61
Fox Gloves 63
Fresh Start 64

Acknowledgments 65

AMBLE

SETTING I
MORNING

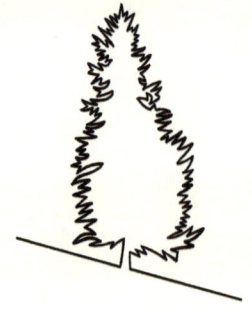

Joy and freedom spreading outward to others

"I must walk toward Oregon."

—from *Walking,* by Henry David Thoreau

Amble

Four walks today on my first trip back in three months.
Four glorious excursions that three times were so slow,
I questioned if they qualified as the same walk.

Moments of bliss so fine I almost dug a hole with my hands
to bury my body in the earth and fall into the sleep of myrtles—

living a full four hundred years, passing through
three major fires recorded in rings.
Strikes of lightning measured nearby
in uprooted trees. If no one is around, correlated by broken crowns.
Tree survival after lightning is not all by chance.
All living creatures have an evolved and buried sense of humor.
Dead trees as bones are poor conductors as electric strands.

My opening eyes flash-stung and blurred in the sunlight
makes me wonder if I am actually an awake myrtle—

the only thought worthwhile to keep in my heart today,
making me feel that maybe, like you,
I am always home here with no need to leave.
My years away are forgiven. I am free
like the minerals in the surrounding soil. We are one.
My steps are an affirmation of my promise. You are not gone.

I Long for the Rain

I long for the rain as one more day finds me. Covered, waterproofed,
pitter-pattered from the first light until my coffee turns cold.

My steps are my part in the day's rhythmic sounding
down the river road and up to the branches to songs in flight.

Home, received, and the sound center—

the dream fulfilled by the mother who told them by every action
seen and all the stories once shared with me and again told,
downstream to the future, infused with a spirit of life-is-fleeting—

play, love, and hope!

Have I kept the path clear for those who come after?

Only the young now will measure, if not with every untrodden dawn
amble, then every heavily sprinkled, late morning walk toward home.

On My Way

I am often pulled into a new idea, as I imagine
an asteroid being influenced by the sun's orbit,
where something is different with each pass and much depends
on what is old in a new space.

Sometimes, an idea moves with me on an unclear path.
Other times, I am so directed on a collision course,
only a chance encounter, with other powerful objects will keep
me from whatever level of absorption
gravity and my place in the universe have before me.

Like every door I pass today on my walk,
I know so many will forever stay closed to me.
On my way to my destination, just one more passing
realization that our world has some ideas
moving us. The universe has taught them many times.

I proceed with my unbalanced mind as it sways in the unseen
stream, while my body, like a careening vessel, coalesces
thought waves with one ear open and collides
with toned-swells of feelings with one eye shut.

Youth-On-Age

In the darkly settled, damp, and ring-counted woods,
sea salt bathed, and mist allured is the home of a Thousand Mothers,
the undying plant, the wise,
earthen one, the lover and model of grounded simplicity.

Both a currant with perishable fruit and a steady *current* of slow-time,
the unchanged, Youth-On-Age, the always with us,
the as-if-cloned, the nighttime story us children were quietly told.

The place of reflection to not be alone,
the refuge from harassing groups' judgment, force, and lonely walks
of shame to home. When arrived—forest-bathed,
open to being handheld, but also happy to roam.

Individually sewn—even as all are alike as on the same thread—

always different too, changing in relation to new forest-neighbors'
acquired—sufficiency through thread-like understanding.

Potted Umbellularia Californica

I grow potted myrtle tree starts to somehow quell missing
home, by capture—
reformed, I now release some of them as gifts to my friends,
those with hearts left here while they are away. The others, through
our shared connection as people reserved and at times even contained.

Knowing the sky was given as a reflection of the ocean without nets.
Living on the land in a world of needs beyond thirst and hunger.
Parlaying my journey's lessons and knowledge, finally
understanding that some joy and community I get by
constraint in exchange for freedom grown and sheared out of license,
a concept that is as hard-earned as it is as lightly maintained since
in each generation, the world is a beguiling place. When you can
no longer return home, not every cry is seen with a tear.

Iris and Home

I have always seen the river valley as a durable basket
or as a hand-woven fishing net, filled
with all the tangible goods to bring to my loved ones at home.
Only improved by what I can glean from the world,
knowing while gone, I walk over a thin, sand-stone bridge,
understanding the outside world is full of straight-cut ideas
to more easily separate by distinctions into all variations of groups.

Returning, always striving to honor and protect the growers,
the we-as-people of the land, and seasonal habit makers. I am cautious
around my past, often well-intentioned, but too power-based and demanding
assertions of good theory over praxis.

I am kind to the learning and naive.
My regrets wrap my fears in the sight of the open-minded ignorant and violent.
I extend an intricate flower to the too easily swept to the root
for simple answers. I am humble in accepting that I could have kettled
with the growers of weakening ties, conformity, and family breakers
as no longer individually weaved together.

I sigh relief that my ideas flew to paper and lightened as I aged.
I only encountered spiritual fishing-net and basket makers retrained,
placed in a false guild, reskilled to fear, and paid in a currency
of what was burned in the darkness of old books
on mechanistic blueprints and fragmented stories of shadow-cave markings.

When safely home, I see friends and family working like the iris, beautifully thriving.
Preserved with woven-spiritedness, branch-rooted
strength and beauty-essence as camouflage.

I take comfort in the privately-held believers in delight-finding through nature
who are engaged from the early morning, prolific in production,
hidden in the towns, while always surprisingly enjoyed
most easily in the forest. When succeeding, wrapping in valley ways
with grass-like beauty. Summer colors shared
through joy and freedom spreading outward to others
the benefits of leaving space for vespertinal grace and evolving knowns.

On the Mountain

Who is the hermit on the mountain?
Are his sounds too light to hear?
The rustling of fabric, as he tends the fire—
steady, short steps, layered with the slight crunching of the duff
forest floor beneath the earth-kissed soles of his feet.
Much like the soft sounds of the world's once roar—
peppered, crackling, blended, yet so muffled and distant,
now, seemingly nothing more than the silence after
a final soft snapping ember's call as spent fuel to its flame.

It is early morning, still dark, and the sun will not rise
for a long while. The coals will persist, but only as a soft charcoal
to find space, where once a warm, healing heat was felt.

Last night, I heard his voice on the wind:

—May the breeze feed the soil for others with all I care that lasts.

When I went to see him today, only dry
coals and the reverberations received of his words in my mind remained
of one more dusk. I saw an unburned root near the fire's edge,
a new start, for an old way of living. I thought of him—
may the wiser wind stir the dust.

I Never Tire of This View

Through all the sights, perfect vision to darkening decline,
I never tire of the tree canyon's view.

Out to the back deck, I always feel held in the embrace
of creased-time, unspoken words of abundance in nature,
fleeting but present, hopeful that I might find space to create
sandstone-creek, iron-filtered understanding, and keep light-hearted
like the gift-color of alder. I bring some times
of joy and release to my loves to better ease their cares.

As the seasons turn, I look forward, even when seeing nothing new.
I follow my dreams as they sail the creek and rise up the canyon
to be welcomed in the tree canopy even though it has no word for *home*.

Hope of Morning

Reaching out, sometimes, painting
a picture of our surroundings with our fingertips.
When we finally get that image, we move to find our place in the world.
Often missing by searching too high or too low. Just doing
the best we can. Bills to pay, family obligations, varying
levels of energy—the canvas for reverberant mistakes we keep making.
Each new day may bring a deeper understanding—
the hope of morning is one more clarifying solution to replenish the dye.

At Our Best

When we are at our best it is as if the world makes sense.
A smile, and a playful shrug, is your answer to my question on how
you slept. We both fall into that first warming sip—
coffee for me, or tea for you,
like two loving parent-birds gliding from our nest
on soft-morning fresh air, buoyantly helping each other
bring sweet nourishment, not only to our loves, but our lives.
Like flowers, we unfold and display with sepal purposes too.

Affirming our space and the opening of our colors—
a tip of your wing my way is an invitation to keep
following you a little longer to meet the sunrise and enjoy
our new day together before finding our way into the world.
You, to your painting, and me, to my writing.
Like the first day we met, when I shared nervously that I was sure
I saw a picture of you in the poem from my dream,
the one that rewrote *me* before the sun rose,
and your revelation, that the night before we met, in your sleep, you painted
a picture with the sound of my voice that was so unexpected and inviting,
the images listened and danced, while *you* leapt to the canvas.

I hope you know that loving day for me is like a blessed poem—
mystical, playful, emotional—leaving me often breathless,
feeling both awed and tear-pressed, richly aware once again the gift
of togetherness is often enjoyed best with those we have long known.

Conduits

I sense them in the first moments of the early morning
return, feeling so real it almost cannot be
merely the shallowest stage of deepest dreams.

Telling me:

—You are both the transmitted and the received.

—Through you, a line—
the infinite to help you more lovingly belong.
Fingertips of the universe,
better to help return and inform what has been felt.

—Some say only to this world, others wonder about the next.

—Seek the place of unforced tears, the place of brittleness and awe.
Where you might shatter to better unform to create the spark
of awareness, the first source of all the old laws that have been sung,
eternally passed through the sounds of the uncounted
others, never fully known, both early and late.

Home and Away

With my books, I am both home and away.
Only my lack of understanding, grounding me to the idea,
discovered anew by every outcast that people are
the deep root that connects a place with time.
As I pass, the pages turn lightly through shared experiences of collected ritual,
found obligations to others, and my conception of the mind.

Infused Path

The path between our homes is a pleasant walk while heading to
an early, still dark-skied, kitchen table-holding hot cup of light
coffee and sometimes surprising, homemade dandelion, mint tea.

I think it is my late morning return home on the narrow,
forest-river infused path with the sun shining my way
from your home to mine, that I am
most aware and grateful that we chose to live next to each other,
rarely ever needing to drive, and even when walking
far away, never leaving home.

SETTING II
AFTERNOON

once again, seeing the rain blowing wildly—

The Complementary Path

I like to walk the shared path each day.
I get to know my neighbors a little better.

I get to see who lives by the checklist—the disciplined ones
who are compelled to act as our seasonal passes of mowing,
planters in rows, and hard-scrabbled maintainers—
efficient, consistent, and spectacular.

And, the ones like me, who aspire to such goals but are easily distracted
by the hot-water-infused coffee and tea—questioners of checklists—
the call to answer the immediate as warm drink and time loaned—
effusive, cordial, and settled.

All the more good-fortuned through our shared blessings—
tolerant, uncompacted-travelers together, as friendly, grateful neighbors.
One branch and two seasons,
for every happy home, often twelve times the unseen support,
like the root area ratio to a crown of a tree,
both leaf and root as our model as complementary souls.

Wind Chimes

The only music I care about on a day like this is the one
produced by the downpour of rain and the expanding
sound across the deck from the beckoning wind chimes.

The ones Grandfather always loved, as sweet-singing,
metal birds, so well. Strung
up on so many of the roof eave perches, like sound
invitations to the back of the house.

The air-dancing ones, yet almost locked in an orbit—
contained, seemingly unpatterned by our lack of time to observe,
hallow calls to calm and reverent contemplation
in the understanding that they take more than one chime to surprise—
another triumph in nature of the few working together.
As I see now, so appealing to one
who felt too lonely by era, choices, and duty to be sound.

As it rains today, I let the water drip in my out-stretched, cupped palms.
Below Grandfather's last-placed metal wind chime, I listen,
images ringing slowly before
once again, seeing the rain blowing wildly—

high in the air, the rain-drops in the wind,
like my memories, filing my vision
with blessings of gratitude for a life rebound.

A received message, every time I sit and hear them in the sturdy rain
as the call to move closer together. Through translation,
finally understanding that my voice finds my day's range best
as part of a choir, with sonorous music that richly fills my mind.

Inspiration is a Spirit

Inspiration is a spirit who most happily visits those who know
it is a precious guest, not just a connection gifted by the accident of birth.

True, some seem to have all the accomplished traits—
knowledge, ease of learning, charm, and complex skills
almost from the start of life, yet there is another
species of genius, which visits later in one's life, sometimes surprisingly,
most often finally accepted, and always more appreciated.

This is the genius of old,
the one we must make ourselves worthy of entertaining.
The spirit of partnered vessels and prepared oracles to speak through.

The one who helped bring you to me,
after all those years, when she changed your voice to playfully enrapture
all who hear you, and let you see,
I was willing to lovingly listen. Even though one person is not a crowd,
sometimes genius needs to be free to create in its moment of discovery—
talent is on time, luck uncovers what is buried by past collisions, turning
what is stored into what is formed. May we deliver what is asked given the sign.

You Like Me As I Like You

You liked my dreams, and we were up all night.
You said you were surprised I felt that way. It could be a bond.
It somehow brought all I had always felt to life and within reach.
All I knew is that I sensed you liked me, as I liked you.

You said you were surprised I felt that way. It could be a bond.
The awareness was authentic, I said, like how I felt about you.
All I knew is that I sensed you liked me, as I liked you.
For me, a different season—like my views, spring flowered and new.

The awareness was authentic, I said, like how I felt about you.
Where do we go from here?
For me, a different season—like my views, spring flowered and new.
Sometimes, life mystically brings before us the most unexpectedly dear.

Where do we go from here?
Sometimes, life mystically brings before us the most unexpectedly dear.
I'd like to go for a walk at the river this afternoon.
You said, "let's stay until dark—the skies are new-mooned and star-mirrored."

That was the first time we kissed.
It somehow brought all I had always felt to life and within reach.
I was there and then continually thankful that you saw what was easy to miss.
You liked my dreams, and we were up all night.

With a Kiss

With a kiss, I have wings, not small, speckled ones
created for precision and utility, but grand, unwieldy,
heavy, the kind you might find on your right shoulder, if you believe
in angels—majestic, pure, timeless, full of promise and unfallen.

In that instant, skyward, one of the few moments of life to always soar.

Then small, once again a tempted, careful,
clip-winged, an earthly broken-bird—

air beating both as a timed sign of the eventual end of this kind
day and the whirling memory of awakening in my first flight, never
to be that high again, yet without regret, knowing
I found more than one way in life to ascend.

Healed

What is a broken heart between friends,
I mean, we both remember the time before,
when all was anticipation, the glory in provisioning,
the general yet blissful ignorance of what comes after.

I suppose some keep the same heart
all of their lives, an enigma if there ever was one.
Some are tragically gifted with a heart
no one wants. Others know not, there is spirit left
to break, by nature or accident's fate.

I wonder if that first, unguarded proclamation is less the first light
from expanding knowledge of the multitude of conversations
or merely the measured shedding of our interpretative soul—

born anew with different harvests, different soils,
nourished by better practices, thriving by what has been
learned, and evolved into what will grow.

Douglas Fir

Each old-growth branch is today's thirty-year harvest.
The pine stands tall with thick bark—old water over spine.
Each handgrip—a challenge to be braver than your friend.
An upside-down world of high death as a home for sight.
Sound is stored for tomorrow's answers, and the mist gives
one last memory of thick forest floors,
as a brief-lived child of the world
headed to a sandy age on ocean floors before
scorched to space together as the end of time.

Bouquet of Nettles

I often take my chances with the nettles on my calves
and the stings on my arms—small, often
painful reminders that necessary moving through even
beautiful spaces is memorably protected
by both nature and what cannot be defined.

I find little comfort as I disturb the silence of misty mornings
or the light sounds of the shedding dusk,
never comfortable as I find life in front of me,

its energies toward living another day, and mine
to deliver freedom from decline, hunger, and obscurity—
the price set by the unflavored ingredient of harvest,
together, part of the bouquet of production for a tea to be born.

Moss Over Wood Ash

In temperate, Pacific Northwest rainforests, old,
round, burnt piles grow over, first, not with grass or weeds,
but a yellow-green moss so soft, comforting, and rug-like, I imagine
they must have once only been
appreciated by the highest attuned or most spirit-gifted.

Wherever located and inhabited, in that instant,
always the center of the universe, receiver
of both the moment's fruit and the future's lost harvest.

By its circular shape, a vector for the eyes of the moon.
By its silence, a setting to absorb soundly orange-sighs of the sun.

Every late fall, I clear a spot in the woods and burn my next brush pile,
knowing once again that the ash will warmly invite the spores
to grow a signal floor to help the world climb away to a sky without shape.

Moss grows over wood ash. Another year is muffled rain.
Soil is memory, buried, latent answers seed tomorrow's health.
My questions overflow into the streams as the world stays on course.

A Good Place for Lunch

Sharing, picnicked, no awkward fear of attracting
the poor and disenfranchised, the vagabond, the car-homed,
the tarp-laden, the bartering and speculation dependent.

Away from a few of the sights I saw on the county logging road today.
The fear of the work gamble—I work, you play, and I die
before I enjoy the same. The feeling of being cheated,
tricked, the dumb one who could not figure out
how to relax and frolic with free time.
The one who never understood that health is the senior joy of wealth.
I plant the garden, you eat the food—I clean up the garbage.
I sweat in the dirt, you laugh behind my back—this place I love crumbles.
You, the one who seems numb or incapable of caring for other's efforts,
get the win—I get the bill.

The perennial problem, the game of strategy,
the challenge of surviving the world one ramble at a time,
where we make assumptions based on appearances—
the sometimes late alter-abled, the too sick, the mentally out-world,
the unhoused who suffer.

Does anyone have the answers?
What is the balance between freedom and license to fall?
My voice carries out of my thin shelter, no concerned eyes on me in my privacy,
only my disturbances ask for silence as my mind demands to be left alone.

The Deeply Hurt Often Fight in Chaos

I remember you as a child, as a teenager,
as one of my students in each of my classrooms—
the agitated one, the moving, the most affected
when something new or unexpected entered our world.

I did not often understand your movements,
your behaviors, your bright-eyed energy. I did not see
the times before at home when you had to move quickly
to avoid hurt, avoid sadness, avoid hunger.

I think I saw you today. After so many years,
I think I know where you have been.
It breaks my heart. I think I saw you in the pictures,
full of collected rage, full of your own escaped oppression.

I mourned your absence of calm, your lack of fullness. You could not stay
still. I wondered if the destructive whirling of your life could have been
any different and if I could have been a better teacher,
a better mentor—someone with more courage to stand with you as a friend.

Life is Precarious

Life if precarious she said, and he believed her as he dodged
his pilot's cough. Life is precious, she said, and he easily ignored
her like an ant's scream. Life is precious, he said, and she adjusted
her designer wool throw. Life is precarious, he said, and at the right time,
she fired 300 employees to hire a friend.

Change of Heart

I saw a change of heart today.
I almost missed it. It was a slight glimmer,
the warmth it created was brief but focused.
My attention caught—all was revealed—
the space around it was dark and ragged in comparison.
I was hungry for its difference. It chose to continue
to feed intelligent life into a system
it did not create but was entrusted with improving and supporting.
It had been challenged and entreated by an old force perceived as new.
A party of conformity of thought, guilt by association, and theory over praxis.

Today, it paused, not out of fear, nor fatigue—
it changed out of truth. It changed out of the beckoning
prayer of friendship, and it reversed
through a gently heard echo of a more common charity.
It lost some of its long infatuations. It recast some of its desire
for that which upon reflection and understanding did not bring revelation—
only reaping and despair. There was a glimmer today, and tomorrow, maybe
an ember to fire the forge to a more versatile understanding
of fragile ingredients. Sometimes even the best systems fail
when outcomes are forced. Love and hate are not materials,
even when cold-dreamers sell them in parts.
Screams are the world's oldest fiat currency.
The new wealth starts with the lie:
The future can only be better through
the fair breaking of today's more settled-hearts that bind.

Flooded Bay

Red is the freshet, or is it blue?
Blue is the logjam, or is it red?
Purple—the flooded bay, sometimes after an election,
where we both cry and laugh at the tension between
freedom and equality and know it will always be so in a constitution
built with both ideas to be true.

I suppose I will just find comfort as the high tide recedes.
Knowing that next time I may go again to unsteady thoughts
if no one hears them, no need for grace. Maybe,
not every solution to a problematic relationship is deeper separation,
not every future calls for more energy and less patience,
not every present is more valuable in proportion to what it erased.

Balance

You, before me—we are tied to place. Memory
to future, down where we walk, all is primarily invisible
like buried dune sand. Anger and fear press our dreams to the past.
Let us optimize our time to have more leisure work to wind
some great ideas to help us all better heal through practiced sutures.

The only magic I have seen in this world to balance what we give
with what we take, with it in abundance, we can
combine equality and freedom to stay more connected.
Some say fools gold, I say—gifted to the lucky as a prized meditation on grace.

Old Dog in the River

I know a type of love that seems to make sense,
a mostly rational love of those who own pets—
love is what we give, not what we get. That is why we pour a small fortune
into keeping them cared for while some of our other wants
and needs are asked to buy time, never met, or are reassigned.

I was not surprised that day when they jumped
in the fast-moving river, after that old, impertinent dog.
The one with only a few weeks left to live.
I was still angry, as I know they knew
the refrain taught to the child who grows up near the water.
Surely they must have remembered
saying it to their children almost every single day.

When he dove for that tired, old dog, in that cold, muddy-weighted river,
he must have just kept his eyes on his friend
and have forgotten to stop, lookup, and stand tall.

Her eyes, no doubt, were on him.
She rushed to catch him as he bobbed quickly away
down that stream. A missed grab and then full awareness,
before that bundle of floating branches swept her beneath all I could see.

Now that I am older, I know love is the only law that breaks all the rules.

Broken hearts are often unbuoyed warnings at the water's edge.

Death is heavier than the combined weight of every lost one's last breath.

Broadleaf Dock

Perennial as the grass, and opportunistically reproducing
mainly by seed. Like other coastal inhabitants,
inclined to make its way in the world in wet and poorly drained areas.

A large mound of foliage is its settled plumage of display.
Rosette-shaped spirit, contemplative, and durable.
Laying prostrate to the ground only to better protect
and support the underused, discounted, and inconspicuous.
Densely packed like its hopes, yet terminal
primarily focused on living and growing undisturbed.

Mature, even flowering in rust-colored panicles.
Brown in the winter, a root's favorite color.
Like other locals, as commonly found in fields,
meadows and pastures, exceptionally pleased
when things are settled and comfortable.

Persistent as the wind on sandstone.
Attached to the home as iron is to water
it drinks to provide nature's irrigation to each bare patch.
The most generous of plants, there is freedom where it can sow.

Pruned Branches

The pruned branches layer the grass,
like my fallen words lay on the page after my first revision.
For me, both are the work of late winter: The branches removed—
room for the sun on the fruit tree—
the fallen words, my sculpted ideas on the ground to grow
a living poem for future harvest.

Together, complementary aesthetics that benefit
from planning and purpose, as precious as the first awareness
of something new, only as perennial as our ability to agree,
a more permanent place is our right through reason's gifts and knowledge
gleaned on the provisioned paths of lives well-lived.

Each day, shaded areas to consider for more light.

Where will it all lead?

I trace the shape of the tree canopy with joy, like reading
fair words of pressed, petal-like contemplation.
Newfound worlds of private, earthy sessions,
the world as the tutor—me, the lucky ink
as the sounds in pulp and methods.

Word Farming

Snapping cable, rocking-chair cut, rilling log deck,
widowmaker and the leg tearing saw,
just a few of the often seasonal concerns from a tree farm.

More ways to cut or kill yourself than forms to read or write.
Less margin for error than your latest,
and maybe your last self-published collection of poems.

Marketable timber for profit as alluring as a six-figure advance
for a hopeful poet's future traditionally published book.

All stiff, saw-chipped, and oil-pressed clothing,
scented of sweat and the late fall molting forest,
fore-father to the pressed page
and cousin to a writer's ink-stained, pen-weary hand.

A word farmers lot, from trees to lumber to perceptions to fall,
building and repairing structures—
the signals of society, still lighted by a desire to hew
a necessary future through the darkness better than the day before.

Both moldable, only limited by the world's capacity
to dream, repair, and keep growing through
the tree farmers' culture and the writers' delight.

Salmonberry and the Next Idea

Broadleaf deciduous shrub, she called me.
—So dense! A stubborn mind, thick as spring-grown brush
and as exceedingly inclined to be prolific in berry wine-made plans
as sparingly branched in safety margins to not go broke.

Shreddy-barked, inclined to shed long-formed plans
in exchange for a quick escape. Prickly when confronted or blamed.
Biennial stemmed, seemingly to just frustrate and hurry on others.
I stay in one place. Lateral shoots only in my obsessions.
Like me, expanding in the same measure as it is annoying.

Lobed and irregularly toothed-grinned so the rest of me can hide
in the shade as the world quickly passes me by.
Born singly in desire for free time but happiest with others
so inclined. Unfolding and expanding,
leaving invitations to slow down the world
like aggregate droplets of tightly packed arguments,
some may fall, but most survive.

Salmon colored to red or reddish-purple in my passion.
Some say it is improving, those I care to know, most
often say lovely, occasionally even, stumbling on the sublime.
All say, somewhat mushy, I think—*I make the time.*

Thimbleberry

Deciduous shrub—climbing or scrambling, like my dreams—
grows the range of human height to better meet the harvest.
Unarmed and inviting, a plant in local style,

lobed in as much as a thought as leaf shape.
Cordate-based by adaptation,
palmately formed, each leaf a wish grown as a gift to the stars.

Serrated as a promise to always clear a path for the gentle.

Crinked, only to share more with others.

Measure of Loss

Today, I still see where to end up.
I have lived away and fought to secure my future stay.
I think I might even have more fear than before.
The talented and fearful ones who leave arrive late.
The talented and brave, who stay, often better know
the truth of good fortune—the place you love is an answer,
all the questions of why are a measure of your loss—
all that live to remember the monumented sky clearly keep the gains.
Wait too long, and see your dreams buried deep by root,
the final, quiet resting place of returns home unsung to the ones gone.

No Trace

Advanced society builds so naturally, I like to imagine
some of what we measure as veins of the rarest, precious
minerals are, in fact, trails through time as technology-erased.

Advanced society can be replaced,
that is its promise and earthen fate,
full of good and bad intentions to venture a new path from home,
still only a lightning-charged tide away forever.
Change is to this world as sand is to stone.
Often a late reminder of life—
only our lack of energy limits our understanding
as our overabundance of fear limits our compassion.

Thinking about a better future is hard to practice,
even knowing and believing takes discipline to sow—one more
borrowed reminder that the only permanence in life is that all is loaned.

A Stop at the Dock

I like to break up all my goings from here to there.
I watch the water pass me by as the tide carries
the long traveled sticks, forgotten
fallen leaves, and my buried, yet altered dreams to the bay.

I hear on the wind:

—Go where I go, and with my goodwill, my friend.

I then remember that the channeled, willow-kissed air has another song
to hold me, and I am called to share my weight to the balance.

My cupped hand is needed here to measure
both reality and what cannot be sensed. Each stop
at this dock is once again my reminder that each day moves, like Avalon,
a little more of my intention and spirit before me. Water-embraced
recognition that we are the world's dream fulfilled,
the children of nature. The ones here to help complete the necessity
of time, both our first awareness and our final
invitation to someday graciously know when to stop.

SETTING III
EVENING

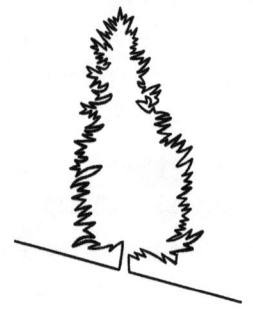

out, sprinting to cover the valley road below. My heart

My Favorite Gift

I give everyday-elegance type wine glasses as wedding gifts—
sturdy, yet refined—the kind that rarely break,
always seem slightly too fancy for daily use, but so fun,
not using them feels like an unthoughtful deprivation and a miserly waste.

I like being happily remembered through the emotional glow
of warm wine feelings and remembered
in heart as a generous provider of the friendly
holder of the essential delicate fruits of play.

I almost hear a whisper of thanks as the glass is selected.
Is that a grateful kiss on the cheek with the first sip?

A walk around the room and a deep sigh is to me, the joy
as if I were your company, with your appreciated,
gentle shoulder squeeze after the first blessed glass is finished.
We haven't spoken in fifteen years.
Like the glasses, I am your durable and unassuming friend.

My gift, as a once generous wedding guest,
may be one of the only things that still truly shines
as if new—much like our untarnished bond—
asking only that you relax into daily contentment and enjoy your wine.

Red, Warm Glare

A red glare in the evening rain, warmly colored, moving,
and then it was gone. After that, I wondered if it was real.
I mean, I did not take a picture, yet it appeared in my sight.
It felt surprising, and it made me recall I once thought I knew it all.

I had always had this idea that for me to stay here,
I would have to be somewhere else first.
When we were together, I was already mostly gone.
Which was not fair to you. Especially when I behaved as if you were
not with me, almost as if you were invisible.

I remember thinking that I knew what you needed—and it was not me,
not then. I was not the perfect vessel for an equally attractive soul.

I was the one you wanted, not knowing
the only way you would ever have the one you deserved was through
someone elsewhere, who like me—never planned to have only one home.

The Gate

I locked the gate to the land passed down to me.
It kept me, the uninvited, and the ill-intentioned opportunists out.
I locked the gate on my summer dream that went unmet,
often mentioned as my future, but always present until it was past.

I was lucky in most ways, sometimes
we are destined to have moving visions,
that which upon still-reflection we know we needed to see.
I suppose time is the first idea to have allowed experiences to be gleaned.

I opened the gate today for my son. He owns the land now.
I wonder if he will see any need for a key?

Ties of Freedom

So many times, we hear about all the things couples must have
or keep in common to have a successful relationship.

Indeed, shared interests are sweet and seem right.
I wonder, though, if too often there is a skewed focus on positive attributes—
liking the same authors, sharing an appreciation
for the same types of music, movies, foods, sports, philosophies,
people, wealth, and having a shared political orientation.

What about the negative attributes that bind us—
fear of poverty, a disdain for the lack of free-time,
anger at dangerous and increasingly pointless work commutes. The minus sum
game of open disgust with the licentious who only have laws for everyone else.

Are not these just as strong, and maybe stronger?

The unlimited interests by subtraction, ties to experiences that cost nothing
and are less about taste and all about hard-earned self-knowledge.
Optimizations gained as joy through overcoming and avoiding. Every pirate
knows, not each shared like always brings love closer together.
Not every salted-spite makes for a brittle bond or an uninteresting home.

Summer Reflection

Today, I saw an attractive image shine brightly off the water,
the warm light reminded me of you, full of joy and mirth.
I could have sworn it was complete with all the love you once had for me.

It was summer, an evening reflection, just slightly
out of reach, hopeful, reminding me of that time
we discovered all of the untrammeled clovers
on the side of that old, cat-logged road, and felt
confident that somehow by doing so, we must have already found
the location of our good fortune—the one we then quickly lost.
The unbroken hearted cannot fairly value whether the first love is the best.

Windfall

A brightening light, a snapping
in the unlocked mind, a clarifying moment of being
present and wholly outside of time, as if for that instant.

Life—its promise of the sweetest joy,
purest acceptance, complete and charitable embrace of all
vulnerability—a windstorm wrought tree, unrooted, yet in touch
with the world, in a way, one never thought possible
to reconnect and grow more expansively, several iterations
of themselves, a rerooting from laying prostrate and courage to grow anew.

Unpaid Carers

The close ones, both expected yet not required.
The caring ones, death by a thousand unseen chores.
Run races like *Pre*—nothing left in the tank.
Take the longest to heal on the shortest path to absolution.

When We Help

Moving that wood was a little more challenging this year.
The same goes for the brush clearing near the house,
which even for me is a hard-clear and long-sweat.
You are still at it with most of the work, as it is with you,
through near misses and health-defying chances.

It felt like we pushed the rusted hinges just a little bit harder this year.
The grass was sheened and the dirt was edged so the place could continue
beautiful, and such a hammocked-joy to all your family and friends who visited.

I think I might finally ask you tomorrow, if not here,
forever, where do you want to be?
The answer might quicken the final projects
to help those who will come after you with some systematic ease.

For now, maybe together,
we can stretch this stewardship journey a little longer.
You can enjoy the continued friendship of a younger, concerned neighbor.
Our proximity, our bond—better sometimes than even your loving family.
Both children of the land—we work in this valley,
heart-glad to help neighbors, clear-eyed.
Another passing of the mantle through earned property-helping peace.
When you leave for the next land, what you loved lives on
through the landscapes I shape and the promises I keep.

Myrtle Trees

After the rain, they stand wide, web-barked, and glistening.
The mature leaves display in evolving colors of fall, covered
with an oil to happily inhale for its fragrant clarifying expression.

The touch of the bark, like a big, friendly pet of a dog
or a sturdy pat on the head of an old, muscled, dust-covered bull,
more in the feeling gleaned than in texture.
If quiet enough and touch with patience, you may even sense them leaving.
We are just another passing leaf below them,
always lightly adding weight to the ground that is too old to care.
Their expanding walls of thin bark are a reminder that nature knows,
even as we become more substantial, we stretch hollow inside.

They are the crack in the veneer of the world, a sight
not complete. A living shell of our perceptions, often as beautiful
as their leaves, which subtly change color and depart in a mixed array.
The old know—not every figured eye at dusk will see
rust colored leaves fall in the unshaped dawn.

Who is Watching the Waves?

This time of year, they sure can lull you in.
A call to the void, if I have ever seen one.
Can I take on that wave and still stand? Will I ever reappear?
It seems a bit safer way back here on the dryer sand. Better viewing too,
if you want to take it all in—oh, what a sight!

Every winter, I come to this very spot.
I marvel at the consistency. It was strange this year,
when that layered, foam-ridden, retreating wave just kept
pulling all the way back and with so much force.

All those school drills, all those white and blue signs with waves—
an arrow pointing to higher ground flashing before me.
All those stories of how they happened in the far past
and will happen again in the far distant future.
The long cycle—it will not get us, not even our kids.

The short, too fast shock that wakes our walking slumber,
the time before—never generous and always early.

I was still not prepared when the waves, slowly
at first, and then heavily thereafter,
started moving me to where I knew not to go.

The world had other plans for me.

I was just watching the waves.
The swells of time disinterestedly counted my tears.
Like every day before, I wondered if I would be gifted
with a tomorrow. At that moment, finally accepted that I had always been
the wave—brief, cresting, and changing as energy restored.

Returning to the Earth

Homes as keepers of the world's old failures are often fairly pedestrian settings.
I never felt those places were necessarily bound to always stay
that way. Where I was, I saw others had also been—
had carried those weights, had repaired that which was
closer to dirt than wood, had rebuilt that which should have been burned.

I saw replaced bricks with stones from our creek.
I saw patched wool clothing made by the best companies of the past.
I saw cedar-ripped lumber, where store-bought flooring could go.

I saw you, never minding, transforming
before my eyes and always close to what you could be,
close to where you would eventually go, wanting for nothing,
somehow knowing and trusting that whole,
grown materials are the experienced and humble ingredients.
Our soul is cousin to the water. The earth is a mixing bowl.

Bald Mountain Meteorite

The evaporated-day was kindle for the star-showered night
in the way chance mysteriously beckons the moving watchful,
who only need the slightest changing winds as an invitation to take flight.
As I suddenly flew past my old home, where my loved ones were
framed in my memories—green colors were behind me, deep in my being,
I took comfort in knowing those I loved (who were gone) were safe
in this garden valley. Now was my time to plant over a remarkable harvest,
that with any luck, no one would ever know was sown.

The sizzling sound was unsettling, a loud
reminder of my mother's stories of her early escape
as a child from ill fortune's streaking chaos and fire,
often shared with us children in times of need and caution:

Some unexpectedly bright calls are otherworldly invitations to land
just below the shallow, root-deep earth as brief answers from the void.
My purpose was clear as a bald mountain.
My hopes that night were as rare as palatite.
That day, a yellow-gem of possibility. All is clear when you have the light.

After carrying the carefully packed, remaining root-wrapped starts
to the end of my journey for a newly planted, myrtle grove—
I was with my loved ones again. Happy, present through
pepper aromas, my life again filled with green and yellow flowered hope.

Healed best in the coastal climate embrace, finally settled and answers known

That evening, I covered the meteor deep as I could with all the dirt from its row,
time-capsuled my sighting in this story with it, planted
my trees and with any luck,
the invocation for privacy will live here as a lesson to those who come after,
a final legacy from my mother, who painfully learned:

Some gems in life are orange-brown warnings of summer, better left buried
for the future in the promise of personal harvests.
Not every feeling of privacy once lost regenerates in the land of its birth.
Land deemed valuable becomes unrecognizable to those who loved it first.

Fox Gloves

Pink, purple, yellow, and white whales on the hill swimming
in yesterday's seas. The silent bells of spring.
Each flower, a thimble to turn each season gently like pages.
Poisonous to stay palatial. Sentinel to succor a tomorrow.
A cresting call to sound an invitation to the day's more watchful sky.
A child's fleet of starships and a parent's lone burial crown.
A model foundation to becoming. Never a sad ending to broken light.

Fresh Start

I see the start line again this evening is still
not cured, just the slightest imprint from that last lap.
With more time it should season.

Good enough to run again, maybe tomorrow I will
get lucky and not think about us. Somehow, I suspect, you will
get past me, but like a new race, we get a fresh start.

The wind racing, a folding in before a blasting
out, sprinting to cover the valley road below. My heart
once again expanding in time to let new love grow.

Acknowledgments

Oregon State Univesity websites provided excellent descriptive terms for many of the plant-based poems. Thank you to the professionals who spend their time and energies updating and sharing core knowledge. The following online resources were particularly helpful:

1) https://landscapeplants.oregonstate.edu

2) https://horticulture.oregonstate.edu

3) https://catalog.extension.oregonstate.edu

Thank you (to my lovely wife), Sarah Craig, who is immensely talented and a key supporter of my writing journey these last few years. She is the author of *The Holiday Window Painting Book*. Her MBA from Western Governors University and her Bachelor of Science in Journalism from the University of Oregon, original artwork, and publishing praxis through Thoughts on the Good Life Press made it possible for this second collection of poems to find its way out into the world.

Thank you to Michael McGriff, author of *Eternal Sentences* (winner of the 2021 Miller William Poetry Prize selected by Billy Collins), and numerous other poetry, writing, and translation work for the excellent list of writing resources and poetry craft insights this last year.

A warm and heartfelt thank you to all my family and friends. We travel together best, even knowing more each year about the value of staying still. And, thank you to all the other lovely people who read my first book: *Coos River Reverberations: Poems of River, Farm & Forest.* Look for more of my invitations to slow down the world.

GUY CRAIG is from Coos Bay, Oregon, where he grew up along the South Fork Coos River. He lives in Tigard, Oregon, and he spends most of his free time in the Coos River Valley.

He holds a Master of Science in Special Education from the University of Oregon and a Bachelor of Science in Psychology from Portland State University. Guy is the author of three other poetry collections: *Coos River Reverberations: Poems of River, Farm & Forest* (2021); *Idling Intuitions: Poems* (2021); and, *Mast Years: Poems* (2022).

Other Books by Thoughts on the Good Life Press

Coos River Reverberations:

Poems of River, Farm & Forest

By Guy Craig

Idling Intuitions: Poems

By Guy Craig

Mast Years: Poems

By Guy Craig

The Holiday Window Painting Book

By Sarah Craig

www.ingramcontent.com/pod-product-compliance
Lightning Source LLC
Chambersburg PA
CBHW060410080526
44583CB00012B/520